For _____

# YOU + ME!

## I LOVE US BECAUSE . . .

### 25 Big (and Little) Ways We're the Best

# 1

# I love us because . . .

I love sharing

_____

with you.

# Because . . .

There's no one else I'd rather

———————————————

with.

I ♥ us
because . . .

We're the perfect mix of

_____

and

_____.

# Gah! And because . . .

Being with you makes me
want to be a better

_____.

# Gosh, because . . .

It's so fun dreaming about

_____

together.

# 6

# We're the best because . . .

It's pretty adorable how we

_____

all the time.

# Oh yeah, and because . . .

I've learned so much about

_____

from hanging out with you.

# Also because . . .

If we were a dance craze,

we'd be

_____.

# And because . . .

I think people secretly wish they were as

_____

as we are.

# 10

I like really, really love us a lot because . . .

One of my happiest memories
(ever!) is when we

_____.

# 11

# And especially because . . .

We always seem to

_____

and we never seem to

_____.

# 12

I love you + me because . . .

The story of how we

_____

is downright

_____.

# 13

I feel lucky to be your person because . . .

I could seriously

_____

with you forever!

# Thank goodness we found each other because . . .

Going

---

with you never gets old.

# 15

# It's crazy
# because . . .

**We always seem to**

_____

**even if**

_____.

# 16

We're kind
of magical
because . . .

If we wanted to, we

could easily

_____.

# We're also pretty charming, because . . .

It's super funny when we

_____.

# 18

I totally love us because . . .

If we were a comfort food,
we'd be

_____.

Or maybe

_____?

# Oh yeah, and because . . .

I'm pretty sure we could

talk about

_____

till the sun comes up.

# 20

Did I mention
I love us?
Because . . .

Watching

_____

with you is just so

_____.

# 21

# And not just because . . .

We've got such fantastic
taste in

_____.

# 22

Thinking about us makes my ♥ melt because . . .

We each always seem to

know just what to

_____

when the other is

_____ .

# Ooh! Because . . .

It's awesome how good we
are at giving each other

_____.

# Aww, and because . . .

I've never had a better time

_____

with anyone on the planet.

# 25

# Because!
# Because!
# Because!

We are so

_____ .

We are so

_____ .

We are so

_____ .

I love us!

# YEAH,
# US!

Created, published, and distributed by Knock Knock
11111 Jefferson Blvd. #5167
Culver City, CA 90231
knockknockstuff.com
Knock Knock is a registered trademark of Knock Knock LLC
Fill in the Love is a registered trademark of Knock Knock LLC

**Fill in the *Love.*®**

ISBN: 978–168349352–5     UPC: 825703–50269–5

20  19  18  17  16  15  14  13  12  11  10  9  8  7  6  5  4  3  2  1